David Cobb

Mounting Shadows

Also by David Cobb:
A Leap in the Light (Equinox, 1991)
ISBN 0-9517103-0-3

David Cobb believes – on the slenderest
evidence – he is descended from a sixth
century Saxon tribe called the Benesingas
(not an ancient pop group) and lives with
a pear tree and a blasted oak in Essex.
He was released from the army with a
testimonial which had only this to say
about him: "He is undoubtedly honest".
In 1991, his haiku gained two international
first prizes, the Mainichi in Tokyo, and
the Cardiff competition, organised by the
Welsh Academy on behalf of Japan Festival
Wales. In Japan he goes by the name of
Kobu, which can be written in characters
meaning "Old Turnip".

Charlotte Smith stables a stuffed giraffe
in somebody else's mansion and once stood
in as a knife-thrower's stooge in an Irish
circus. She survives in Essex.

Mounting Shadows

David Cobb

EQUINOX PRESS

Author's Note: Charlotte Smith's brush drawings were much admired in my previous book, and I am delighted that she has thrown in her lot with me for a second time.

For earlier publication of some of these poems I thank the editors of Bare Bones, Blithe Spirit, Dragonfly, Frogpond, Haiku Canada, Haiku Quarterly, Iron, Ko, Mainichi Daily News, Modern Haiku, New Welsh Review, Periaktos, Quartos, The Rialto, and Woodnotes. And particularly Kevin Bailey.

For translating some of my poems, I thank Marianne Kiauta, Carl-Heinz Kurz, Koko Kato and Ion Codrescu.

Also, for their special encouragement and stimulation, I wish to mention James, James again, Charlotte, Marianne, Meriel, Kazue, Stephen, and my family.

British Library Cataloguing-in-Publication Data
A catalogue record for this book is available from the British Library.
ISBN 0-9517103-1-1

Published in 1992 by Equinox Press,
Sinodun House, Shalford, Braintree, Essex CM7 5HN

Design and Typeset by Ray Owen

Printed by Higham Press Ltd, Shirland Derby DE5 6BP

Orders in North America to: PO Box 313, La Honda, CA 94020, USA
Orders in Japan to Ko-no-kai, 1-36-7 Ishada-cho, Mizuho-ku, Nagoya 467

IN THE VALE OF PANT

drawing the curtains

on bare poplars   to see rooks

        wheeling behind them

such power –

     three sparrows to a twig

        holding the wind down!

in the vale of pant

---

half of the glisten

is pussy willow – half

late winter rain

on a jet of crap

the blackbird is propelled

from worm to worm

the first kiss of rain

has given this sleeping pond

the April pox

a rook alighting

finds some spring in the bough

of the brittle oak

a leaf still trembling

    after the thrush has vanished

      with its song

      that mystery again:

      the pear tree whitens as

            the blackthorn greens

one tilt of a wing

and the falcon sweeps away

to the end of the wind

a bumble bee

weaves through the ribbons

of the maypole dance

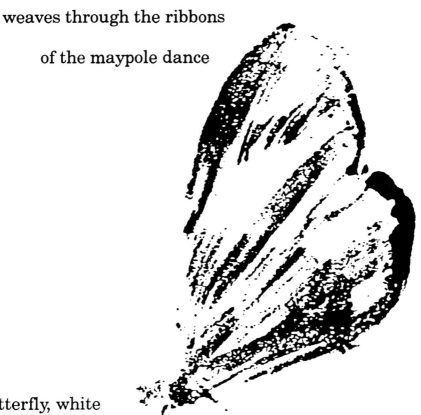

a butterfly, white

sips from a dungpile, and

departs still white ...

in the vale of pant

---

in summer haze

absolute to the skyline

    linseed blue

      repeatedly

      the pigeon trips to the pool

      tipping in pebbles

grasshopper –

how it leaps, leaving

    the greenness!

peacock butterflies –

on cosmeas so many

as to make them bend

the watering can

swinging

from side   to side

censing geraniums

night chill

through the damp nappy

to the mother's cheek

dead-ending

the hung rose —

showered with raindrops

midsummer's day:

bee and gardener toiling

as the darkness fails

no time to shave

the farmhand setting out

to reap the corn

a white butterfly

without visible concern

falls to a wagtail

bronzed

under the gypsies' hedge

a Christmas tree

back from holidays:

    heads of water lilies

        crane from the pond

                two butterflies track

                their shadows to a leaf

                and mount them there

across the fields of stubble

    flame   stalks   flame

in the vale of pant

---

talons at the heart

of robin's territory

in the digger's arm

gypsies evicted –

in the ditch, for kindling

a broken chair

a bright New Year's Day–

the sexton cuts clean edges

in the soft firm clay

---

    the frost holds:

    Friesians in the byre

    chew steam

starlings – mobbing

the slow, infrequent drip

from an icicle

in the vale of pant

---

any second now

the hole in the road will sprout

a blue tattoo

                    the mist is rising

                    even

                    under the lowered

                    coffin

traffic snarl

along the motorway

kestrel to kestrel

even when crushed

in the overtaking lane –

    the fox's ears

                the hunt is out:

                a man in red on a horse

                by a clamp of swedes

an old man crouches

under a damson tree

loading a spray gun

harvest almost won:

by the last stands of barley

farmers with guns

pinchpenny –

he's even ploughing in

his own barbed wire

23

the street vendor's cry

twisting the leaves off

wilted lettuces

for all his stamping

the market boy has crushed

not a single fly

under the laden pear

an abject pensioner

is gathering windfalls

the seagull squints

both sides of the sea wall

into brown bosoms

at the turkey barn

security lights glint

in a fox's eyes

the one path not ploughed

goes to the barn where

souvenirs are sold

the killing fields of essex

the postman's fingers

jumbling in bleak midwinter

two classes of mail

under the signature

the faint watermark

of a fish

minding the robots

technicians shift their weight

from foot to foot

                              I had a girlfriend

                              who used to live here, he says,

                              and taps the TV

everyone reads it,

she says, scratching her acne –

the Kharmasutra

last tick of summer –

the widow moves the hands

to a new curfew

a pair of pheasants

wing from the beater's cry ...

a brace of pheasants

the neighbours plant

another Twelfth Night tree

behind my maples

SPECTRES

hoarfrost:

   a red sun setting

          on

*   an ultimatum

* 15th January 1991

the ex-serviceman

holding a tray of matches

may have heard one struck

    an ivy tendril

runs over the statue's face

    meets one on its spine

still whinging

all round the white men's graves –

mosquitoes

around the war cross

shadows of old comrades

immersed in puddles

turning from her grave

the tug of a rose thorn

on my padded sleeve

at the amateur

Hamlet dress rehearsal –

Yorick's real skull

one foot on the style

again I'm with my father

picking mushrooms

there goes the man

carrying a bag of bowls

who digs our graves

harvest barn-dance:

now with the village sexton

do-si-do

(father wears a sling

on the mortuary slab

to mend his grin)

old battlefield:

hail pouncing

on the scattered cairns

Flanders – few inches

between death in summer

and death in the spring

almost unobserved

   a flabby balloon leaks out

      a breath of Old Year ...

doctor's typewriter

stutters over the r's

of a referral

after the snowman

melts into the lawn –

picking up his smile

a diffuse smoke

from old Dove Cottage chimney

mingles with drizzle

FENNEL FOR JAPAN

Remembrance Day fair –

a little cricket chirrups

in a bamboo cage

at the ryokan tap

the face she has worn all day

is washed away

this downpour

has blinded even the god

who brings the rain

on the pavement side

kimonoed in pink tissue

and laid neat – a turd

tremors in Tokyo –

municipal workmen hoe

the flowerbeds

airing the pillows

showing the guest the cloud

blanketing Fuji

where the distant peak

should rest upon the shore-line –

storm-whipped water

how they bow – those frogs!

meeting on the limelit path

neglecting the fly

the sun reflecting

on the ice reflecting

on the frozen sun

the tinkle of wind chimes tumbling maple leaves

LETTING THE MOON GO FIRST

                              prayer, prayer –

                              the jackdaw croaking

                              at al-Aqsa mosque

copper-bottomed

ladies in bermudas

being camel-humped

at Charlie's end

        of the plane   the rose clouds

                              are losing height

making a peg-leg

for a friend, the leper

grips with a scar

at the Chinese wake

pale lotuses in the lake

draining a pig

now, north of the Alps

ten words are reckoned

conversation

on the way to home

we wait by the narrow bridge

for the moon to pass

TWO AND TWO

two persons only

chatter above the tube din —

deaf, and signing ...

umbrella'd lovers —

   the rain falling, briefly

     on both their backs

two and two

---

daily we meet:

always she wears a smile

going the other way

her skirt swings open

to envelop

lavender

sealing with lips

self-addressed envelopes:

sometimes sweet glue

two and two

---

posted to Holland

in the middle of your name

a flake of snow

white and pink

in the tide pool

nails and toes

on the open moor

some seeds of ling implanted

in her parted legs

two and two

hands in the shared book

move with the teacher's question:

"Love – regular verb?"

           homewards bound

                 moon

           moonwards bound

                 home

           the web I can't see

           but I'm infatuated

           with its one loose strand

---

homecoming:

a two-day growth of beard

bristles her nipple...

a spider swings

across her forehead

on an auburn strand

two buzzards

mewing as they pare

the skin of a cloud

ONE IS ONE

coming down

through lark-song, my daughter

on a parachute

                         horned cattle:

                         a boy driving them home

                         into long shadows

whelks

all over the beach

auntie's bunions

how mercilessly

the nightingale sings   in mauve

to a darkened heart...

lice home from school –

everyone washing their heads

except the poet

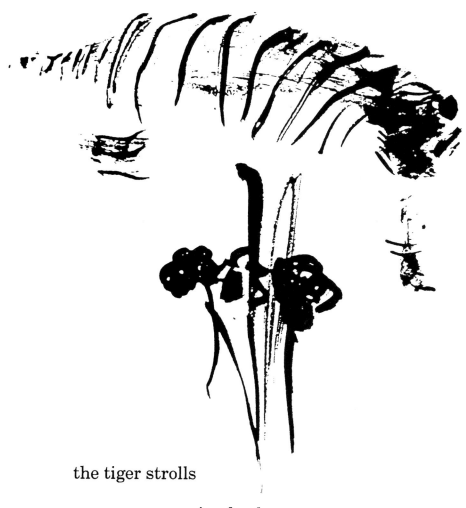

the tiger strolls

on spring heels

round some daffodils

---

above the hundreds

of rooks in an oak, one rook

half a mile high

now a crane-fly

tramples my concentration

on the window pane

haiku workshop:

the novice's name is tied

to her walking stick

hurrying home

after the haiku workshop –

harvest moon

the moon's hugeness

reflected

in the small girl's eyes

torches and the frost:

one of the carol singers

caught not singing

DO YOU SPEAK GOLDFISH?

look, a lugworm

angling its golden tunnel

towards France ...

            it's no use mouthing

            O after O at me –

            I don't speak Goldfish!

the fledgeling squeaks

    when feet it meant to tap

        ....begin to run!

into the mountain

goes the bit of the crane-fly

she lays her eggs with

born

swallowed:

guppy fry

even on my thumb

the crawling ladybirds

continue mating

swans' wings

whirring too slowly for bodies

to catch up heads

do you speak goldfish?

while he drills my teeth

trying to work his nose out

and his twisted smile

this longest night

the dog cocks half an ear

towards the stars

the chocolate grin

adores the dandelion

in the tulip bed

SMALLER STILL AND SMALLER

briefly on the kale

the shade of a butterfly

collapses its wings

the days shorten —

dim through the window, buds

of chrysanthemums

in the flower-pot

waiting to be transplanted —

thistledown

swirling round

the mirrored alder tree –

the alder's leaves

---

at Christmas time

the wheelbarrow still full

of unemptied leaves

bleak snow:

following foottracks to

the perished robin

this morning

the aprilness

of lean sparrows

---

feather in beak

one sparrow on the phone wire

steps into air ...

                                        on-shore breeze

                                        cold-wet on my leg

                                        the spaniel's lick

a walk in the hills:

across my sandwich the wind

                    streaking the bacon

pedalling uphill

a butterfly

overtakes me

pedalling uphill

into the smell

of pigs

slowly the sun

has turned the windmill's sails

from west to east

after buddleia

the butterfly zigzags

across the zebra

well into dusk

the bee labours

on a fading bloom

end of summer:

the patio table

folded in two

smaller still and smaller

---

in the crumbling porch

wild bees are storing honey

before evensong

the cuckoo flies

copying recopying

its hunted echo

within the shadow

of the blossoming tree

my shadow